READING AND LINGUISTIC DEVELOPMENT

by

Paula Menyuk

Boston University

Volume 4 in the series
From Reading Research to Practice

Brookline Books

ISBN 1-57129-071-0

Library of Congress Cataloging-In-Publication Data
Menyuk, Paula.
    Reading and linguistic development / by Paula Menyuk.
        p.   cm. – (From reading research to practice ; v. 4)
    Includes bibliographical references (p.   )
    ISBN 1-57129-071-0
    1. Language acquisition.   2. Reading.   3. Cognition in children.
I. Title. II. Series.
P118.M424   1999
401'.93–dc21   99-11226
                                                                    CIP

Book design and typography by Erica L. Schultz.

Printed in USA
10   9   8   7   6   5   4   3   2   1

Published by
BROOKLINE BOOKS
P.O. Box 1047
Cambridge, Massachusetts 02238
Order toll-free: 1-800-666-BOOK

Contents

Preface .... *iv*

Introduction *1*

Chapter One *6*
Language Development Over the Preschool Years:
Curriculum Implications

Chapter Two *17*
Language Development Over the Early School Years:
Curriculum Implications

Chapter Three *49*
Language Development Over the Later School Years:
Curriculum Development

References *56*

About the Author *59*

Preface

In this book — part of a new series, *From Reading Research to Practice* — Paula Menyuk brings to classroom teachers of reading the important research findings on language development that have been reported in scientific and professional writings during the past two decades. These are reported in non-technical language to make it possible for teachers to use the knowledge to help their students.

Reading and Linguistic Development is concerned not only with the language development of middle-class children, but also with that of children from varying cultural and linguistic backgrounds and of those who have developmental language problems. Classroom teachers will especially appreciate this comprehensive view.

At the beginning the teacher is introduced to a model of how oral language knowledge plays a crucial role in the acquisition of reading, and how reading changes during sequential periods of development — preschool, early grades, middle grades, and high school. Special emphasis is placed on the early grades because the most dramatic changes in language development occur then. For each period, differences due to social and biological factors are considered. And throughout the book, teachers learn what educational and clinical activities can support and enrich student language development at all levels.

This book by a noted linguist brings to those who work in reading an understanding that is sorely needed at this particular time.

Jeanne S. Chall, Ph.D., *Series Editor*
John F. Onofrey, *Editor*

Introduction

Research in language development has blossomed over the past two decades. We now know much more not only about language development in white middle-class children but also about this process in children from diverse cultural and language backgrounds, as well as those with developmental anomalies. Because much of this research is reported in technical papers and books, it is difficult for pre-service teachers and clinicians – as well as those already involved in these activities – to access these findings. Further, it is not always clear what impact this information should have on work that will be done and is being done with these children. Therefore, the purpose of this work is to provide some needed introductory information on language development and to try to make clear the educational consequences of this information.

In the introduction I will present a model of how oral language knowledge plays a crucial role in the acquisition of reading. This model proposes that awareness of all the categories and relations in language is of primary importance in learning how to read. In addition, some theoretical positions frequently found in the literature about the role of nature versus nurture in this development, and the relation between cognitive development and language development, will be discussed. Then we will examine language development during sequential periods of development: Preschool, Early grades, Middle grades, and High school. Emphasis will be on the early years of development because the most dramatic changes in language development occur in that period. There will be a brief discussion of variations in developments due to social and biological factors during each period. Finally, we will discuss information about educational and clinical activities that can support and enrich language development during these periods.*

---

*   The Menyuk et al. studies reported on herein were partially funded by a grant from the National Institute of Deafness and Other Communication Disorders (DC00537) awarded to the author.

The Role of Awareness in Reading

It has long been held that learning to read involves knowledge of the following various aspects of language:

(1) the speech sound system (phonology);
(2) the meanings of words (lexicon);
(3) how words are put together in utterances to convey a message (semantics and syntax, or as some have termed it, semantax); and
(4) how discourse or conversational interaction of varying kinds is carried out (pragmatics).

The beginning reader, usually aged five or six years, has an enormous amount of knowledge of language, but is, for the most part, unaware of what he or she knows. There is evidence that children at a younger age can be made aware of certain aspects of oral language with which they are familiar. For example, children three years of age or even younger can be asked to judge whether a sentence is "okay," to rhyme words, and to put sounds together to make a word. A number of studies have indicated that by age three children will be able to judge that the sentence "ball the roll" is funny, that the word *lap* "rhymes with" (sounds like) *cap* and *map*, and that the three sounds /k/a/t/ when put together become *cat* (Menyuk, 1988).

In the reading process, one of the earliest developments of awareness of the relation between print and spoken language is the child's request to be told what this "says." In the writing process, one of the earliest behaviors beyond scribbling and picture drawing is the request to have "my name spelled." These are the beginning stages of finding letter-sound correspondences. Once engaged in more formal beginning reading programs, the child may point to a written word and sound it out letter by letter or may simply remember what the whole word says from a previous experience. Both processes, sounding out and recognition, require awareness of the relation between what is on the page (the printed word) and a linguistic representation of the word (oral speech). That linguistic representation includes what the word sounds like and what it means. That process is represented in Figure 1.

As shown, the child first focuses on the word — that is, *categorizes* the word. Then he or she brings to conscious awareness or *decodes* either a sequence of sounds (as in /k/a/t/) and then *translates* this into the word /kat/ and *produces*

Figure 1: Steps in achieving awareness of a word when reading.

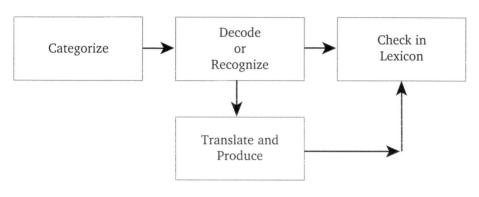

it, or simply recognizes the word /kat/ and produces it. In either case the child brings to conscious awareness either the sound composition of the word or the whole word. Then the child *checks the meaning in the lexicon.* This is a translation of what is on the page into an oral language word that is known. Whether sounding out, recognizing or using picture or context cues to guess, the child *produces* the word and relates the sound sequence to its meaning by checking in the lexicon. This process requires bringing to awareness both the sounds and the meaning of a particular word. At some later stage of development this process becomes *automatic* and the child no longer needs to be consciously aware of the relation between the printed word and its phonology and the meaning of the word stored in memory. This is indicated in Figure 1 by the direct arrow between the "decode/recognize" box and the "check in lexicon" box, bypassing the "translation" box. But until the process becomes automatic, the translation and overt production steps are needed before the word can be checked in the child's lexicon.

This process of initially bringing aspects of the text to awareness continues as children become more adept readers. When the child is reading sentences, he or she becomes aware of the relations among the words in the sentence, and brings to awareness semantactic knowledge or what the words and their arrangement mean. When reading connected discourse, the child brings to awareness pragmatic knowledge — that is, how conversations and stories are organized, what is included in descriptions and explanations, etc. Thus, awareness of aspects of language knowledge is required during the beginning stages of each developmental change to more and more sophisticated reading, and then the process becomes increasingly automatic. However, even well-practiced readers, when reading difficult text about subject matter that is unfamiliar to them, will once more call upon awareness of lexical, semantactic, and pragmatic knowledge to help clarify the text. They may even sound out unfamiliar words to check and see whether it is in their lexicon. In addition to linguistic knowledge, and awareness, world knowledge also plays an important role in reading comprehension. However, a great deal of world knowledge is acquired via linguistic knowledge, awareness and reading. Therefore, one other aspect of learning how to read and to read well is dependent on language knowledge and awareness. These findings, obviously, have implications for teaching of reading. Teachers need to teach and to use materials that have language structures and vocabulary with which children are familiar. They should do the same when talking about new areas of world knowledge that are in the readers.

Some Theories About Language Development

To simplify a great deal, current theories about language acquisition seem to be divided into two camps, traditionally labelled "nature" and "nurture." The term *nature* implies that language development is innate, dependent on the biology of the child. *Nurture* implies that this development is largely dependent on input from the environment.

Steve Pinker (1994) describes his view of how language is acquired and used in a book that the *New York Times* described as "brilliant, witty, and altogether satisfying." Both the book's title, *The Language Instinct,* and its subtitle, *How the Mind Creates Language,* emphasize the role of the human nervous system with its built-in abilities in the acquisition and use of language. Thus, the nature camp seems well represented by this book. All students of the process of language acquisition would agree to the importance of the human infant's biological competence, compared with that of other animals, in providing the raw material necessary for the acquisition of language as we know it. Although other animals communicate, no other species has language as linguists define it. No other animal has a system of communication composed of several levels of units (signs or sounds, words, sentences, and discourse) from which unique combinations of units are created, and then used to converse and theorize.

However, the degree to which language development is thought to be affected by nurture (environmental input) varies among researchers. There are some who suggest that both the home and the school play a critical role in the process. Thus, even though nurture does not affect the acquisition of knowledge of the grammar of a language (that is, all normally developing children will acquire the sounds and words of their language and rules needed to create unique utterances), input can affect its richness (the amount of units acquired within each subsystem, e.g., number and types of words) and certainly its variety of uses.

Among educators and clinicians there is general acceptance of the nature versus nurture aspects of this controversy. That is, there is general acceptance of the fact that children are unique in their abilities to acquire a language as is indicated by both differences between them and other animals in communication, and by the effect of various biological differences such as brain damage. However, the child's home and school experiences can contribute in important ways to language development and use. Clinical interventions can be very helpful for children who for various biological reasons differ from others in their knowledge and use of language.

In another controversy, philosophers, psychologists, and linguists have debated the role of cognitive development in the acquisition of language, and conversely, the role of language in cognitive acquisitions. One widely debated issue is whether language development is part of cognitive development — the so-called "connectionist" view (that all systems of knowledge are connected) — or independent of it, the "modular" view (that systems of development are separate from each other). The continuing debate makes it clear that this is an unresolved issue. Some psychologists such as Vygotsky (1962) hold that words are required for first organizing (separating from each other) and categorizing (seeing similarities between) objects and events in the world, and then conceptualizing about (seeing relations) among these objects and events. Piaget, on the other hand, held that the growth of logical thinking, underlying sensorimotor development, is a necessary precursor to the acquisition of words (Piaget, 1970). Further, said Piaget, this acquisition was only one symbol system, a way of representing the world to categorize objects and events (drawing would be an example of another way). Further aspects of language development — e.g., markers of tense (past, present, past participle, etc.), number (singular and plural) and comparison (of objects, for example bigger and biggest) — would also be dependent on the further development of logical thinking. However, once language has been acquired, its importance in vital cognitive processes such as conceptual development and memory has been subject to little debate (Seigler, 1991).

Chapter One

Language Development Over the Preschool Years: Curriculum Implications

Over the first five to six years of life, a child rapidly acquires substantial knowledge about all aspects of language. At 18 months, the average child has a comprehension vocabulary of about 100 words and a spoken vocabulary of about 50 words. By age two and a half, the average child is able to produce over 500 words. At two years the average child comprehends subject-verb-object relations in sentences (who did what to whom, e.g., "Big Bird kisses Cookie Monster"), and is responding very appropriately, if minimally, in conversational interaction. The reply to "Do you want an orange?" might be "Yes" or "No, I want a banana." During the third year of life a very dramatic growth in vocabulary occurs. Sentences uttered by the child become more adult-like in their structure; that is, they tend to follow the rules of the language more frequently than not. For example, a two-year-old might question a statement by saying "That be bird?" A three-year-old might sometimes say "Is that is a bird?" and sometimes "Is that a bird?" By four years of age, non-grammatical versions of questions have disappeared. Now the child produces both simple and complex sentences that contain markers of relations among the words such as articles, adjectives, and markers of plural and tense. An 18-month-old child might say "Daddy" or "Daddy go?" A four-year-old might say, "There's a boy, sleeping in the field, and a big bird comes and wakes him up."

Table 1 on the next page summarizes the structural developments that occur at pivotal points over the first five years of life: 18 months, 3 years, and 5 years. This outline indicates what children can be expected to produce and understand, on average, at these ages. Remarkable changes occur over these years in all aspects of the language, and these changes are all in the direction of acquiring the structures that are in the grammar of their language. As shown, developments occur both in comprehension and in production of language,

Table 1: Language development in the preschool years.

	Age	Comprehension	Production
Vocabulary	18 months	100 words	50 words
	36 months	4,000 words	2,000 words
	60 months	8,000 words	5,000 words
Syntax	18 months	S-V-O relations "Baby Kisses Mommy"	Two Part sentences "Baby kiss"; "Kiss mommy"
	36 months	Simple and Complex "I know that's a bird"	Simple and Complex "That's a bird?"
	60 months	Conjoined and embedded sentences of all types	
Phonology	18 months	Top / Pop	Top=pop, Pop=pop
	36 months	All speech sounds	All singleton speech sounds
	60 months	All speech sounds	Most speech sounds except some clusters
Morphology	18 months	"Two book"	"Two book"
	36 months	Markers of number and tense	Errors: "Childrensiz," "Camed"
	60 months	Some derivational markers (ex: "-er")	Some derivational markers

but early on there is a large gap between the two abilities. As children mature these abilities approximate each other more closely, although substantial gaps continue. The gap between lexical comprehension and production abilities, in particular, is quite wide throughout the school years. At the earliest ages there is a close tie between language production, memory, and psychomotor abilities (that is, articulation movements). For example, the child may be able to combine two or three words into one sentence but only does so with hesitations between words and slowly. He or she and may drop off a word because of a strain on memory retrieval and because articulating them takes so long. Articulation movements require a highly skilled motor development, and this motor development is part of the biological repertoire of normally developing children. As the child matures, the rate at which he or she speaks increases, and spoken sentences become longer.

In addition to acquiring the grammatical rules of the language, the child also acquires the rules of conversation and discourse, the pragmatic rules. These rules are especially important in terms of "fitting in" with the expectations of the school environment. A book entitled *Way With Words* (Heath, 1983) puts forth, in great detail, the role that preschool experiences in communication interaction play in terms of readiness to interact according to school's expectations. Of particular importance are the rules for listening and turn-taking. Table 2 below presents a summary of pragmatic developments that occur over the five-year period before formal schooling begins. As Table 2 indicates, the

Table 2: Pragmatics development.

Speech Acts	Age	Stage of development
Requests for action	18 months	(in context) non-grammatical: "Pick up"
	36 months	grammatical: "Pick it up!"
	60 months	"I want you to pick it up."
Requests for information	18 months	(in context) non-grammatical: "All gone?"
	36 months	grammatical: "Is it all gone?
	60 months	"Can you tell me if it's all gone?"
Commands	18 months	non-grammatical: "Gimme cookie"
	36 months	grammatical: "Give me a cookie," and some politeness: "please"
	60 months	modal: "You must give me a cookie"; polite requests: "Will you please give me a cookie?"
Statements	18 months	(in context) non-grammatical: "That bird."
	36 months	grammatical: "That's a bird."
	60 months	All types of comments
Discourse	18 months	Taking a turn (begins much earlier)
	36 months	Short, often non-cohesive stories; appropriate responding but frequent topic switching in conversation
	60 months	Greater topic following but still switches; longer, still non-cohesive, stories

requirements of conversation and discourse take a longer time to master than the grammatical components of language.

It should also be noted that some pragmatic abilities are dependent on grammatical competencies as well as specific discourse abilities. For example, polite requests depend on the ability to generate questions ("Will you pass the salt?"). Pragmatic development relies heavily on the ability to observe and reproduce the cultural conditions for discourse as well as on structural competence. Pragmatic abilities include the appropriate use of the paralinguistic cues of intonation, stress, gesture and facial expression. Different cultures indicate varying degrees of politeness by the use of these cues in conjunction with particular language expressions. Thus, what might be considered impolite in one culture is considered polite in another. For example, establishing eye contact with the person addressing you, regardless of their status in relation to you, is considered polite in our culture, but impolite in a number of cultures when the person you are addressing is of a superior status.

Various theories have been proposed to account for these very rapid changes in language knowledge. One theory, the innatist theory discussed earlier, proposes that the child has the genetic equipment to develop language that follows the rules of the adult language of the community, and will do so as long as the child is biologically intact. In fact, this theory suggests that there would need to be substantial differences from normal in the child's nervous system to prevent this from happening (Pinker, 1984). Other theories suggest that the child has the ability to process the language heard or seen (deaf children acquire sign language) in ways that allow him or her to develop language (MacWhinney, 1982). Perceptual and memorial abilities unique to humans allow the child to derive the rules of the native language. What appears to be generally accepted is that language cannot be acquired simply by the imitation of models supplied by the adults in the child's environment. Many reasons have been put forth for not accepting modeling and imitation as an explanation for this development. Foremost among these reasons is the fact that the child produces utterances that are never modeled. It would take many lifetimes to be exposed to sufficient instances of all the different types of sentences that are possible in the language and then to memorize each of these sentences.

Both the innatist theory and the theory suggesting that the child's special processing abilities bring about developmental changes in language knowledge hold the position that the largest share of the language acquisition task belongs to the child. It is the child's unique linguistic and/or cognitive abilities that make language acquisition possible. The child needs to be exposed to language in order to acquire it, but beyond exposure to language, the role of input is unclear. Those of us who are concerned with the role of education in language development need to clarify the role of input in the process. It has been argued that one role the environment might play is to simplify the data for the child in various ways so that the units that make up language, and how these units are related, might become evident to the language-learning child. For example, although it has been found that children do not learn how to ask questions simply by repeated exposure to them, the conditions under which they hear (or see, in sign language) questions, clarify the ways in which questions can be put in their native language. Usually emphasis is placed on the first word in questions (for example, *"Did* he go?"; *"Can* he come?").

However, a distinction is made by many child language researchers between acquisition of grammatical knowledge (the categories and rules of the language, such as how to ask questions) and knowledge of how to use language. This latter knowledge, without argument, is dependent on input to the child — that is, how language is used in the child's community. Children acquiring different languages acquire somewhat different grammatical rules. For example, children learning English learn the rule of putting auxiliaries and modals in front of the sentence in questions, as in the examples above, whereas French-speaking children learn the form of *"Est-ce que."* However, the claim is that children learn a set of grammatical rules of their language in similar ways — a combination of innate abilities, linguistic and cognitive — and that some rules are universal across languages. Rules of use of the language, on the other hand (for example, the degree of politeness used in asking questions, the situations in which questions are asked and of whom), differ markedly among different sociocultural communities. These arguments are of interest to educators because both what children learn about language and how they learn it has implications for language education in school.

Research has shown that speaking simple, short sentences to the child — or so-called "motherese" — has little effect on the rate at which young children acquire the grammatical rules of the language (Menyuk, 1988; Menyuk, Liebergott, & Schultz, 1995). What appears to be more important in the development of both grammatical knowledge and knowledge of how to use the rules of the language is the *type* of discourse (conversational interaction) that takes place between caregivers and young children. In the discussion of curriculum implications, some findings concerning simplifying the context for language learning will be discussed at greater length. Although different sociocultural groups within a society engage in different kinds of discourse with children, all societies have a special way of interacting with young children. In our country, the ways in which middle-income families interact with children may differ from the ways of lower SES (socio-economic status) groups (Heath, 1983). However, in all societies, what is provided in these interactions are "appropriate" ways to interact and opportunities to interact (Schieffelin & Ochs, 1986). In these ways children can deduce the structural rules of the language and learn the pragmatic rules of the group.

The Multilingual Experience

Infants who are exposed to more than one language during these early years acquire the vocabulary and grammar of their two (or more) languages. The differences that may exist in these children's knowledge of language has been the focus of increasing attention as the number of children with multilinguistic backgrounds entering school in the United States increases each year. There are varying theories about what takes place throughout these early years in terms of knowledge of each language (Bialystok, 1991). One theory suggests that one language dominates during the very early months of life and that the dominant language is the one heard most frequently. Other theories suggest that the two languages are intertwined from the earliest months and that each language affects the other from the beginning. Logically, the pattern of bilingual development should be affected by the frequency with which each language is addressed to the child. However, other socio-linguistic factors may play a role as well, such as the value a particular culture places on a particular language. During the process of development, although there is constant code-switching from one language to the other, the infant always keeps the two languages separate but selects from each language aspects of the speech sound system, lexicon and grammar that are the easiest for him or her to acquire (Genesee, 1989).

Given these differences in language experience, there may be initial delays in the acquisition of the two systems of language. However, by the time the truly bilingual child enters school, he or she has sufficient knowledge of the two languages to function well academically in either language. This is not the case with children who enter school with limited knowledge of the language dominant in the school. The degree of knowledge of the two or more languages that a child will develop over these early months can be affected by the sociocultural background of the child (Krashen, 1996). These differences may lead to lack of readiness to handle those academic tasks that require well established knowledge of a language. Some of the cognitive advantages that are believed to be a product of bilingualism may not develop because these children may not be advanced sufficiently in their knowledge of the two or more languages they are learning. There have been many arguments about cognitive advantage in bilingualism which will be discussed in a later section on language development in school aged children.

Language Problems

During these early months of development, certain conditions may lead to a greater or lesser delay in the acquisition of the child's native language. Some of these differences may be quite apparent, such as retardation or cerebral palsy. Deafness may preclude initial acquisition of a spoken language, but not of a signed one. In addition to these obvious conditions, some children may experience more or less marked delays in language development for reasons that are more difficult to detect, such as mild or moderate hearing loss or particular language perception and production problems. For example, a population of children has been found that are markedly delayed in language expression. At about 18 months of age, most children have on average about 50 spoken words. Shortly thereafter, a vocabulary spurt occurs; the number of new words they produce increases very rapidly. However, a small number of children do not experience a spurt at age two years. Some of these children continue to be delayed at three years and still others at four (Rescorla, Roberts, & Dahlsgaard, 1997). While many of these children appear to catch up at four years of age, some recent research suggests that these children may experience reading difficulties as they enter school (Paul, Muncy, Clancy, & Andrews, 1997).

Similarly, children who have had many episodes of middle ear disease during which their hearing is affected may also suffer difficulties in reading acquisition because of the effects of a fluctuating hearing loss on their language perception caused by periodic ear infections (otitis media). It is not clear that a language deficit results directly from this kind of loss. A reasonable position appears to be that the condition may lead to problems if other detrimental factors occur in addition to the otitis media. For example, a poor early education experience together with chronic otitis media may negatively affect the child's language development (Roberts, Sanyal, & Burchinal, 1986).

Curriculum Implications

Children are enrolled in various kinds of educational programs at very early ages. In the past, preschool programs started at three years; today, many provide child care for the infants of working mothers. These preschool programs vary in quality. Among other things, there appears to be a direct relation between the number of adults to children and how well the program fosters development in general and language development in particular. This is a crucial factor.

The most important factor in moving the child along in terms of language acquisition during these early years is the amount of opportunity provided by caregivers for children to participate in conversational interaction. These opportunities are provided by mothers at the earliest ages as they participate with their infants in taking turns vocalizing with each other. For example, the mother may say "Hi, baby," while face to face with the infant; the infant responds by saying "ah" or "oo"; and so on.

Somewhat later the infant "participates" with the caregiver as mothers give their children what are called proto-directives. For example:

> The mother directs the child to roll the ball. The child picks up the ball. The mother says, "Yes, pick up the ball." Or the child picks up the cup and the mother says, "Yes, pick up the cup."

These exchanges serve two roles. The first is affectual, with mother affirming what the child is doing. The second provides help in vocabulary development: the mother is naming the object that the child is focused on. This is an instance of *joint attention*. Somewhat later interactions require more sophisticated responses. When the mother says "Roll the ball," the child is expected to do so. Still later, when the mother says "Do you want a banana?", a "yes" or "no" or some other appropriate response ("banana," "apple," etc.) is expected. Expectations grow in these exchanges as the child gives evidence of being able to understand and to respond.

A situation similar to those of joint attention are what are called *contingent responses*. When a child points to an object and attempts to name it, the caregiver responds appropriately by affirmation — not inappropriately by changing the subject. A contingent response to the child pointing up and saying "bird" is "Yes, it's a bird" (or "plane" if it is one), not, for example, "Look at the car."

In summary, there are four kinds of caregiver behaviors that seem to move language development along during this early period. They are:

(1) Providing ample opportunities for communicative interaction.
(2) Talking about what has the child's attention.
(3) Requiring more sophisticated responses when the child gives evidence of being able to be more sophisticated.
(4) Being contingent in interactions to affirm the child's naming of objects or events.

These behaviors have been referred to as *scaffolding* or *providing supports for* the child's early language acquisition.

Children ages three to five years have achieved a great deal in terms of syntax, vocabulary, and phonology. Conversations and stories read and told about familiar experiences can help children learn more about language, especially more about lexicon (vocabulary). Being read to early and often also plays a very important role in the development of literacy. The literature on emergent literacy, or the experiences that lead to formal reading (Teale & Sulzby, 1986), makes it very clear that children who are read to from the earliest months of life begin to exhibit literate behaviors early on. Thus, literacy development, a crucial component of education, depends on two aspects of preschool experience: the development of knowledge of oral language and how to use it to communicate and to learn about the environment, and early and repeated exposure to print.

A combination of print exposure and communication about that print further enhances oral language and literacy development. Early print exposure may involve repeated readings of simple texts while pointing to pictures. Later readings involve not only repeated readings but also discussions about the content of the text, and relating that content to the experiences of the child. Communication interaction about text helps in the development of *print awareness*, that is, the understanding that print represents language. Just as oral language interactions become more complex as the child matures, so do written language interactions.

The implication for curriculum with children of multilingual backgrounds is to provide both communication interaction and print experiences in the language that is familiar to the child. Much has been written, both pro and con, about "bilingual education" (Krashen, 1996). A recent dissertation (Homza, 1995) studied first-graders who were being taught to become literate both in their native language and in English. The successes these children achieved in literacy indicated that acceptance of oral and written language in both the languages of the child, and simultaneous exposure to oral and written forms of these two languages, produced good results. Innovative preschool programs in which children who are competent in a language other than English are taught English and their peers who are native speakers of English are taught the language of the non-English speakers (two-way bilingual programs) are generating bilingualism and biliteracy by the students in the classroom.

Children who have language development problems due to mild or moderate hearing loss, children who are "late talkers," and children with so-called specific language impairment (SLI) are usually integrated into the regular classroom. Although children with moderate hearing loss are usually, but not always, identified during the early preschool years, the latter two groups are usually not identified until later, around age three, when standard tests of language development can be used. Currently, an early assessment instrument of vocabulary development can be useful in determining which children are delayed in language development (Fenson et al., 1993). However, since this instrument is a checklist for parents to complete, it relies heavily on their cooperation.

Children with hearing problems *need* to be in a well-lit, quiet setting in order to benefit from the experiences in the classroom. This is not easy to accomplish, as any preschool teacher knows. A great deal of useful information can be obtained from the audiologist who has tested the child's hearing on how to arrange the environment effectively and from the speech pathologist on intervention techniques to help these children process the speech signal. The speech pathologist can also provide helpful suggestions regarding any children who are experiencing a delay in language development. As was stated earlier, being read to frequently is good for all children, but it is especially so for children with language problems. Frequent reading and rereading of books is an important source for stimulating the development of all aspects of language. Such experience can also help these children to learn to read.

Children who experience delays in oral language development also frequently experience delays in learning how to read (Menyuk & Chesnick, 1997). In particular, these children tend to have difficulty figuring out the relation between letters and sounds, or *decoding*. A great deal of experience in developing phonological awareness of the segments in words can prove extremely useful in helping these children overcome their problems in decoding. During the preschool years, all children can be engaged in a number of activities that help in developing phonological awareness: (1) rhyming games, (2) thinking about words that begin and end with the same sound, (3) putting separated syllables and sounds together in words, and (4) thinking about what is left when parts of words are removed.

Children with language problems may have particular difficulty in this area and, therefore, need a greater amount of practice than that required by the rest of the class. For all children, with or without these problems, the activities should take place with meaningful material — but this is especially important for children with language problems, who rely very heavily on meaning to determine the more abstract components of words. For example, children are much more successful at putting sequences of syllables and sounds together when the result is a meaningful word (/k/a/t/ is easier to put together than /k/ a/f/), and can talk about what is left when what is left is a real word (when /s/ is taken away from "spit" is easier than when /s/ is taken away from "stim").

Chapter Two

Language Development Over the Early School Years: Curriculum Implications

In the United States and Canada as well as most of Western Europe, formal schooling begins at six or seven years of age. For developmental reasons, formal schooling before that time is considered unwise. These developmental reasons involve the ability to attend and to sit still for the amount of time considered necessary to learn to read and write, do mathematics, and study science and social studies. Although children may vary markedly in their interests and abilities in these areas, the belief is that, on average, they are ready to participate in these activities at age six or seven. Those children who have had lots of preschool experiences, in the home and in the school, in activities that have prepared them for the more formal aspects of schooling, are more ready to participate in the enterprise. By first grade a normally developing child knows an enormous amount about language and about how to use language to achieve various goals, both social and academic.

By this age, children have a great deal of experience in using language to determine the meaning of lexical items (vocabulary) they might not have known before, and the meaning of connected discourse (oral scripts and stories) by using their grammatical knowledge and the context. These abilities allow children to be ready to store and retrieve information in all the academic areas, since this information is presented to them primarily through language (lectures and texts). They are also able to use the learning strategies of rehearsal and semantic categorization, since they have had a great deal of practice in using these abilities to acquire the knowledge of language and of the world that they have already achieved. In addition, children this age can use language to form concepts by examining the relations within a chunk of information (some have called this semantic networking; Case & Okamoto, 1996) and to solve problems that are posed in all academic areas by "talking" their way through these problems. Language is constantly used in school to learn about the physical and social world (Menyuk, 1988). Finally, language is used to learn to read, a skill that provides a powerful linguistic window to further knowledge and to recall.

At the beginning of the elementary school years, one facet of language in which there is sizable empirical knowledge is vocabulary. Various researchers have come up with somewhat different numbers, but one frequently referenced study (Templin, 1957) reported that first graders had a basic recognition median vocabulary of 7,800 to 13,000 words. In addition to vocabulary knowledge, they know how to recognize and produce the speech sounds and speech sound rules of their language. They can, for example, discriminate between native and non-native speakers of their language, and they know that combinations of /st/ and /sm/ at the beginnings of words are permissible in English, but not /sr/. Further, they have acquired knowledge of the fundamental syntactic rules of the language. They both comprehend and produce utterances that follow these basic rules, and can detect errors in syntax in those structures they are familiar with. They can participate in coherent and appropriate conversations on a number of topics. Although they can engage in connected discourse such as story telling or a short explanation of how to play a game, this connected discourse is, initially, not well put together. In essence, children of school age come with knowledge of the grammar of their language and of how to use this knowledge. Theoretically, most children come to school with all the linguistic knowledge that is needed to begin to engage in formal education. However, when the language of the school is different from the language they know in structure and in use, they are less prepared. If they have language problems, they are even less prepared.

Despite the fact that children know a great deal about language in grade 1, they learn a great deal more over the school years. Certainly, vocabulary grows enormously. A recent study of vocabulary development from grades 1 to 5 indicates that children have a vocabulary of approximately 10,000 words at the end of grade 1 and a vocabulary of about 40,000 words in grade 5 (Anglin, 1993). This researcher suggests that the enormous leap in vocabulary is due to the ability of children to understand relations between root words and derived words. Derived words are those that are composed of stems and prefixes, suffixes, or infixes. For example, the derived word *baker* is composed of the base word *bake* and the morphological ending *-er* meaning "one who." The word *unhappy* is derived from the word *happy* plus the prefix *un-* meaning "not." The word *historical* is derived from the word *history* plus an infixed stress shift from the first to second syllable, laxing of the vowel /ē/ to /i/ in the final syllable, and addition of the ending *-cal.* The first two types of derivation are understood much earlier in the school years than the last, because the last changes the internal structure of the words. Because children gain implicit knowledge and then awareness of the relations between stem and derived words, they can rapidly add to their comprehension vocabularies. Anglin estimates that children's vocabulary knowledge grows at the rate of approximately 20 words per day over grades 1 through 5.

There are many other dramatic changes that occur in language knowledge during the early school years. For example, in knowledge of how to combine words in spoken sentences, there are marked changes in both the complexity and length of the utterances produced. Children begin to use many more sentences that combine (conjoin and embed) sentences. Before first grade, the typical conjoined sentences are produced by stringing thoughts together, yielding sentences such as "I played with Tommy and I wanted to play with Billy and we went to the park and we all played together" or "He didn't want to play with me so I didn't want to play with him so I played in the park." Early embedded sentences are usually infinitival or participial in form: "I want to play with Billy" or "I like playing with Billy." In first grade children are ready to use more complex conjoined and embedded sentences, but they seldom do so unless they are involved in lengthier discourse activities such as story telling or "sharing" time. Given this reluctance, children need to be encouraged to combine sentences in various ways. Such sentence combining activities can be encouraged in both spoken and written language by asking children to think of different ways in which two sentences can be put together. This, of course, helps in understanding the complex sentences sometimes found in text. Table 3 on the next page lists the marked changes that occur in the conjoined and embedded sentences produced and sometimes understood by children, as well as the rough order in which these changes in complexity appear to take place. Comprehension of complex structures precedes production. These developments indicate that, for the most part, children grow in their ability to produce and understand the relations expressed in sentences by moving actors, actions and objects around rather than keeping them in the fixed order of actor–action–object. These data can be helpful in planning the order in which sentence combining activities might be presented.

The other marked changes that occur over the school years are those con-

Table 3: Development of conjunction and embedding over the early school years (from simpler to more complex conceptual structures).

Conjunction
I see the boy and the girl.
The boy and the girl are sitting at their desks.
Joe sang and danced in the school show.
I like playing the drums and the trumpet too.

Embedding
I like the boy who sits next to me.
The boy who sits next to me is my friend.
The boy the girl hit ran into the yard.
Joe promised Susie to play with her.

cerned with pragmatic knowledge — that is, how to use language appropriately when speaking with others. Children in conversation with others begin to understand the necessity of making clear who and what they are referring to so that their listeners will understand what they are talking about. The seven-year-old may tell you a story about a squirrel and refer to the squirrel and other characters in the story as "he" without clarifying which "he" is being referred to. They also may plunge into the story without providing sufficient background information. They may begin with a statement such as, "The squirrel tried to get enough nuts." Ten-year-old children do not do this to such a great extent and adolescents to an even lesser extent (Hickmann, 1985).

Examples of stories by preschool (age 4), early school (age 7), and later school (age 10) children were obtained by Hickmann after they viewed a film. The differences among their stories make clear the changes that occur over these early school years.

Preschool:

"Penny was in the box. The penny was in the box. The next day it wasn't. He was mad at the giraffe ... 'cause he took the penny, yeah but he di–bu-but he–he thought he was tricking him ... see b-because ... bec–bec–he–he–didn't know that he had the penny. They went to go play."

Early School:

"She was mad ... because his—her penny ...was lost ... and she thought he took it ... and he said, 'Maybe you left it at school.' Then they went to school and got the penny. And that's all."

Later School:

"A donkey and a giraffe came out. And the giraffe said, 'Hi! Would you like to play with me?' And the donkey said, 'No! I'm mad!' And she said, 'What happened?' ... and the donkey said, 'Well, I made a box to keep my things in, and I found a penny. And I put it in the blo-box but now I can't find the penny.' And the giraffe said, 'Well, maybe it's at school! Remember ? You took it to school.' And the donkey said, 'How do you know? I think you're the one that took the penny!' And the giraffe said ... um ... 'No, I didn't.' And ... Oh, she said, 'How do you know?' He said, 'Well, you know, I remember you took it.' And then she thought about it for a while and she said, 'Well, friends don't steal! I'm sorry I was mad at you! Now let's go play.'"

In these examples, not only does fluency increase and sentence structures improve, but greater coherence allows the listener to follow the story and comprehend its structure. This greater clarity in story telling does not seem so much a matter of being able to take the other's perspective, as Piagetians contend, but rather to result from increased linguistic competence. Further, the use of cohesive devices in story telling may be the result of increased knowledge of the structure of stories, and how they are told. This skill has probably improved because of the many experiences the children have had in listening to stories read to them or told to them and in attempting to tell their own stories. The conclusion that "... friends don't steal!" is a value acquired from many sources: literature read and viewed, and conversation.

In addition to story telling improving with age, the topics in peer conversations and child–adult conversations also change over the school years, as does children's ability to interpret underlying meanings or make inferences about the content of conversations (Dorval & Eckerman, 1984). Both these evolving abilities, the ability to formulate discourse in a clear and informative manner and the ability to more adequately interpret and make inferences from discourse, have been explained by Piaget as being due to the increasing ability to take the perspective of the other, that is, the ability to keep in mind what the person addressed knows (Flavell, 1985). Thus, changes in pragmatic abilities have been ascribed by some to increasing cognitive abilities. Others suggest these developmental changes are due to changes in social ability, i.e., increasing experience in how to tell stories to others and in how to engage in conversations with others. Still others suggest that increasing linguistic competence *per se* allows the child to use language in these more effective ways. It seems reasonable to suggest that these three developing competences — cognitive, social and linguistic — are all needed, and all contribute to these changes in pragmatic abilities.

Pragmatic competence requires good memorial abilities. The speaker must keep a great deal of information in mind simultaneously: the status of the addressee, the rules of the language, the rules of the culture, situational factors (for example, how noisy the environment is will affect how loudly the voice is used), and the past history of the conversation, as well as where he or she wishes the conversation to go. These factors make clear why it takes a quite a long time to develop appropriate conversational skills. The amount of experience in participating in conversations can have an obvious effect, but reading texts in which conversations take place can add to the experience gained in spontaneous discourse.

The other area of language development in which marked changes occur over the school years is in the awareness of the linguistic categories and relations in all areas of the language: lexical, semantactic, phonological, and pragmatic. Developmental changes in awareness of linguistic categories and relations manifest themselves in at least three different ways.

First, the particular categories and relations that children are aware of change as increasing knowledge of the language is acquired. An example of this change is that children may be aware of what a good subject and predicate of a sentence are before they are aware of what a good relative clause is. Thus, at age two they may think sentences such as "Ball the roll" are "funny" (Gleitman, Gleitman, & Shipley, 1972). At age six they know that the former sentence is wrong and, in addition that sentences such as "I like the pajamas what my mother buys me" are also wrong.

Second, the level of awareness deepens. They can more quickly become aware of more aspects of language as they mature. For example, at age two they think for a while and say that the first sentence above, "Ball the roll," is funny semantically. At age six they know that both the first and second sentence are wrong syntactically (or structurally), and they tell you so quickly.

Third, the ability to talk about awareness of a category emerges. This third ability is manifest at about age 8. Children are capable of telling you *why* both of these sentences are wrong and, in addition, may be able to correct them.

The above examples show changes in awareness in the semantactic area. Very clear examples of changes in awareness also occur in terms of morphology. Obviously, the two-year-old does not understand the relation between *happy* and *unhappy* but does understand the relation between *birthday* and *birthday cake* and between *baby* and *baby monkey* (Berko-Gleason, 1958). The preschool child understands the relation between *bake* and *baker,* but not the relation between *sign* and *signal* or *sane* and *sanity.* The first grader is beginning to understand these relations and can even understand that the derivation of *baker* is different from that of *hammer.* However, it is not until the later grades that the relations between stems and derived words are understood, errors in form detected, and such errors corrected (Menyuk, 1991). First comes intuitive knowledge of categories and relations, then a budding awareness of the category or relation, followed by full awareness, and finally the ability to use this awareness to judge good instances and correct bad instances (Karmiloff-Smith, 1986). These latter abilities are important in producing understandable stories and explanations, both spoken and written.

When writing, the writer clearly needs to bring to conscious awareness many aspects of his or her language knowledge as the process of writing takes place. Before they begin school, some young writers have been observed to produce *invented spelling,* the result of directly translating what the words sound like into written letters. Some delightful examples of invented spelling are the following: "pals" for *palace,* "butr" for *butter,* and "botl" for *bottle.* These spellings follow the rule that final syllables can be represented by a single letter, because they sound like letters (*s, r* and *l,* respectively). Early writing has been described as "writing what you say." To do this, the writer brings to conscious awareness *what he says.* Awareness is particularly important in a crucial aspect of good writing: editing text after it has been generated. This process often causes the writer to speak, vocally or sub-vocally, the text that has been written.

Awareness in spoken language units changes with maturation. I observed examples of the changing nature of awareness during a study of sentence repetition abilities in children at ages 3, 5, and 7. Some of the sentences given were correct and others incorrect. One of the incorrect sentences was "I see tree." The following are typical responses from children of various ages when they were asked whether "I see tree" was right or wrong.

Age 3: "It's wrong because you can't say that."

Age 5: "It's wrong because you can say I see Billy. But you can't say I see tree."

Age 7: "It's wrong because you've got to say I see *a* tree. You can say I see Mary or Jane, but you have to say I see *a* tree or *a* glass."

After exposure to grammar instruction, children will learn to state that nouns that are proper names don't require an article while common nouns do, and that singular nouns can take the article *a* while plural ones require *the*. However, one can see in the answer of the seven-year-old that children of this age are becoming aware of the principle, but are still unable to express it in terms of a "rule." The child starts out with an intuitive feeling that the sentence is wrong and then is able to state what is wrong by providing examples of right and wrong utterances. Finally, the child is able to provide examples of classes of words that do and do not require articles. Still later the child will be able to talk about the differences between classes of words that do and do not require articles. Engaging children in activities that require awareness of language at the different levels helps develop awareness of language at all these levels and, what's more, is fun.

We started out by saying that first-graders know a great deal about their language and about how to use it. However, we have also indicated that over the early school years children learn a great deal more about their language. Table 4 on the next page summarizes the findings that have been obtained about the development of language knowledge over the early school years.

Clearly, learning to read and write plays a crucial role in the further development of the child's linguistic knowledge. Most children learn these skills in school. Therefore, schooling plays a critical role in the development of reading and writing competence and, in this way at least, a crucial role in the further development of language. A child who can read will learn a great deal more about all aspects of oral language: phonological, lexical, semantactic, and pragmatic. Reading allows reflection about language, since in written language words do not disappear; they remain and can be reviewed and thought about. However, it will be argued here that oral language development *per se* plays a crucial role in the acquisition and development of reading and writing. Therefore, oral language development must occur both independently of reading and writing development, and also in a symbiotic relation with reading and writing development. Several papers in a collection on reading acquisition and problems (Grimm & Skowronek, 1993) attempt to explicate this symbiotic relation at the

Table 4: Lanuguage development from first grade to fifth grade.

Skill		Grade 1	Grade 5
Vocabulary	*Recognition*	10,000 words	40,000 words
	Production	4,000 to 5,000 words	8,000 words
Syntax	*Comprehension*	All the simple and complex rules	
	Production	All the simple rules	Most of the complex rules
Phonology		All the speech sound discriminations the language requires	
Morphology		All the rules for number and tense, PLUS some derivation	Most of the rules of derivation
Pragmatics		How to converse and tell stories	How to explain and argue; how to take the perspective of the other

phonological level: that is, phonological awareness is necessary for decoding, but decoding is an aid to phonological awareness. In fact, such symbiotic relations exist at all levels of the language (Menyuk & Chesnick, 1997).

It has been pointed out by a number of researchers that the reading processes of word recognition, comprehension of connected discourse, comprehension monitoring, and inference all require language knowledge and awareness of language (Menyuk, 1984; Perfetti & McCutchen, 1987; Vellutino, 1979). The crucial role of linguistic factors in learning to read and to write and in the ongoing development of reading and writing is indisputable. Further, it is reasonable to state that the development of language in the ways that have been touched upon in this brief overview depends on the development of reading and writing. However, continuous development of aspects of language depends on school activities other than reading and writing. What happens in the classroom — in terms of oral language interactions within the classroom and school, communication between teacher and student and among students — can also affect language development and, by extension, affect development of reading and writing. These relations between language knowledge, reading and writing, and school experiences are represented in Figure 2 on the next page.

Figure 2: Relations among language development, reading and writing development, and schooling.

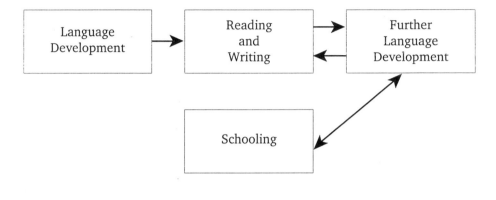

Curriculum Development

Given the above argument, it is important to examine the school activities that may have a profound effect on further language development. What will be emphasized are two factors that are important in curriculum planning. First, there are some activities that appear to lead to the acquisition of *further knowledge of language,* and some activities that lead to the development of *awareness of categories and relations in language.* Although various activities can promote these different achievements, both types of activities lead to the development of language knowledge that plays an enormously important role in academic accomplishments. Second, both types of activities need to be congruent with the present level of development of the child's language, and at the same time challenging enough to move the child along in development. Vygotsky (1962) has characterized such activities as being within the child's "zone of proximal development," or ZPD. The theory of the ZPD is that guidance from someone more expert than the learner can help learning in all areas.

Communication Interaction to Further Language Development

Helping the child achieve greater competence in language knowledge and language use is one goal of curriculum planning. However, the achievement of this goal is crucial to successful performance in all aspects of learning: mathematics, science, social studies, etc. The question remains: how can this be achieved? As discussed above, there have been many studies of mother-child communicative interaction and the influence of this interaction on children's language development. Although the exact role of these interactions remains debatable, most studies have agreed upon two conclusions. First, the mothers of the young infants studied created some conditions under which language categories and relations were more easily distinguishable, such as asking the babies to do things that they were already doing (protodirectives) and, in this way, providing labels for objects or activities they were already attending to. Second, they provided opportunities for participation in communication and acknowledgment of participation. One condition that was clarifying was that mothers talked about the "here and now" rather than the "there, before and after." This apparently was of great help in understanding the meaning of words and ongoing actions. The frequency of these behaviors among different mothers was clearly related to the rate at which children progressed in vocabulary development and in participation in conversation.

There was great interest in the results of these studies on the part of preschool educators and clinicians. However, a number of questions were raised about the applicability of findings concerning child-directed, one-on-one speech in the home to an elementary classroom setting. Wells (1983) compared communication interaction in the home and in the school and found that even in kindergarten and the early grades, the topics of conversation varied markedly between home and school. Further, the conversations that took place in the school were teacher-organized and followed a format dictated by the teacher. Whenever deviations from that format occurred, teachers tried to get the children "back on track" or rejected responses that did not follow their design. Some of these differences between home and school conversations seem necessary, while others do not. The school setting is different from the home setting in many ways, and to some extent, communication interactions in the home and school are carried out for different purposes. However, some of the findings — about the positive effects of clarifying reference in interactions by talking about what the child is focused on rather than changing the topic, allowing opportunity for the child to participate in interaction rather then just passively listening, and acknowledging such participation when it does occur — seem very appropriate applications in the school setting. Further, there is a great deal of evidence now that classroom discourse can lead to better knowledge of the topic being studied by the class (Edwards, 1993).

Some types of interactions that take place in classrooms have been criticized by researchers because (1) children are required to listen quietly for long periods of time in some classrooms without any opportunity to participate, and (2) interactions with teachers may consist primarily of responses to questions, and these questions may only require a "yes" or "no" or other one-word response (Mishler, 1975). Although the contexts and the purposes of these interactions differ in the school and home, it is felt that some aspects of home interaction should be carried over into the school. Beyond providing opportunities for interaction, these opportunities should be authentic rather than contrived; the motivation for communication should be clear. Asking the kinds of questions that children know the teacher knows the answer to is not authentic. Asking yes-no questions or questions that require a one-word response does not provide sufficient opportunity for exchange of ideas. Authentic-question–based curricula prevent students from having to participate in what has been termed a "switchboard" mode of interaction, in which teachers ask one-word-answer questions and children only respond to these questions. Instead, such curricula are designed to encourage the teacher in the role of "inquiry facilitator" rather than just "knowledge transmitter." The following discussion highlights some school activities that have been found by researchers to fulfill these requirements. Oral language school activities which allow communication interaction to take place will vary with the age of the children and the nature of the curriculum, but some generalizations can be made.

First, activities should provide models of more sophisticated language use. Although these activities need to be congruent with the children's linguistic knowledge and developmental interests, sentences that are more complex and are connected in more complex ways than the children ordinarily use can be presented.

Second, children should be allowed to exercise their increased knowledge of the language. There are two types of listening and speaking activities which seem very appropriate for the classroom setting and may be related to other academic content areas. These are narration and explanation or exposition.

Narration is one area that has recently been studied a great deal with children during the earliest school years. Story reading and story telling model connected discourse, provide children with exemplars of more complex sentence structures, and expose them to additional vocabulary and its use. These dual activities provide increased information about all aspects of the language: pragmatic, semantactic, lexical, and phonological. As mentioned earlier, children in first grade still have a great deal to learn about the form of connected discourse as well as about topics for discussion outside of their own immediate experiences. Story reading and story telling may be familiar activities for some children and not for others. However, these activities will be a valuable help to all children in the further development of language, and of great interest to them.

To encourage interaction and to provide an opportunity for exercise of increased knowledge, spontaneous story telling and retelling of read and told stories by the child have been employed. Recent research on the narrative abilities of children indicates two things. First, there are clear developmental changes that occur in story telling, both in the structure of the stories themselves and in the language used. Second, exposure to story reading and telling by others has a significant effect on both these aspects of story telling (Berman & Slobin, 1994). Not only does experience in listening to stories and telling them lead to further development of oral language competence (e.g., discourse competence), but also this increased knowledge is apparently related to the development of literacy skills. Perhaps this occurs because many of the texts that the children read in the primary grades have a narrative structure. The development of a notion of story grammar or structure leads to better comprehension of text that has this structure. Further, there are topics in subject areas, such as history, which seem highly appropriate to talk about using a narrative structure. Thus, children can be simultaneously engaged in developing their discourse skills, their literacy skills, and their knowledge of a subject area such as history or, perhaps, the history of science.

Language arts texts propose a variety of language listening and language production activities that are designed to teach specific listening and speaking skills. Giving speeches or public speaking seems prominent among the suggestions made. This seems a reasonable suggestion as children move into the later grades and develop the necessary language skills to engage in such discourse. However, the purposes of public speaking are multiple, and the possible topics are myriad. Teachers need to consider these issues and investigate how both topic and purpose might be designed to fit the abilities of younger as well as older children. "Show and tell" activities in the earlier grades can be used to help children develop their ability to describe (an adventure or object) and to explain (how a new toy or computer program works). Science is also part of the elementary grades curriculum. The teacher can model description and explanation in this subject area and then ask the children to provide their descriptions and explanations of the same and different topics. Topics in social studies and in mathematics as well as science can also serve as themes. In the older grades as well as the younger, description and explanation can be related to the other academic activities in which the children are engaged. For example, an explanation or exposition on a specific theme in science might be appropriate for a presentation followed by a discussion by the students — not only in the science class but in the language arts class as well.

Like narrative, explanation or exposition has a structure. That structure is quite different from narrative structure and requires expertise in organization beyond a sequential arrangement of events. Main ideas and their development is the principal structure of exposition. Studies have indicated that children are able to comprehend the structure of narratives long before they are able to understand those of exposition (Richgels, McGee, Lomax, & Sheard, 1987). Much of the text material that older students encounter has an expositional structure, but children initially may have difficulty understanding the structure of this type of text. Understanding both the content and the structure of a piece of expository writing facilitates its comprehension, just as was the case with narrative structures.

By modelling the narrative structure through reading and retelling activities, teachers can positively affect the structure of stories told by children. In a similar way, modelling expositional discourse can help in the development of an understanding of its unique structure and positively affect oral description and explanation. Just as story telling and retelling can improve children's comprehension of the structure of narratives in text, modelling expositional discourse helps children develop an understanding of its structure in text. Later opportunities to exercise this newly acquired knowledge can be provided by a series of expositions to the class for further discussion. Moreover, the teacher does not need to be the sole model; older students or peers who have received special training can also be used (Cazden et al., 1978). Familiarity with the structure of exposition enhances the comprehension of the materials and texts that children have to read in all subject areas. Thus, these activities improve comprehension of text across the curriculum.

Much of the emphasis in the above discussion was placed on the encouragement of children's connected discourse skills, which in turn could be used in both oral language development and the comprehension of written text. These activities, however, can also play an important role in the development of conversational skills. It has been suggested that conversational abilities develop in two ways over the school years. One way is in the changing nature of *topics* of conversation. Interactions in the classroom that are based on authentic questions from the academic areas about the physical and social world can enrich the topics of conversation within and outside of the classroom. Interactions based on authentic questions also provides practice in the second area of development of conversational interaction: *taking the perspective of the other.* Differing views on appropriate answers to questions engage students to listen to and understand their peers' responses to questions, as well as to think about their own. Participation in group activities that require connected discourse and conversational interaction help children develop fluency in those skills. Such participation encourages a more frequent use of complex sentence structures and of new vocabulary which is increasingly composed of derived words. Thus, not only pragmatic skills, but also skills in the production of semantactic, lexical and phonological categories and relations in the language, can be developed in the classroom.

The following examples of two conversations are taken from the Dorval and Eckerman study (1984). These conversations were elicited from students of various school ages who participated in a group session for which no particular topic was provided. As these conversations demonstrate, younger children need guidance in getting started and keeping a topic of conversation going, while older children need less. It is also clear from these conversations that as children mature they are more able to stick to the topic, more able to take the perspective of the other, and able to use more sophisticated language. Just getting children to talk *more* in class isn't sufficient to accomplish the linguistic and academic goals of classroom discussion. Discussion must be carefully planned and guided; only then will practice in classroom discussion lead to more expertise in classroom discussion.

In the conversations presented below each utterance in the conversation is numbered to indicate the order in which they occurred. As can be seen some utterances are responses to a previous utterance while others introduce a new topic. This is especially the case in the early conversation.

Early conversation:
1: "You talk too much!"
2: "Poopy pants!"
1: "Big mouth! Big mouth!"
3: "Walk funny girl!"

4:   "I was riding my minibike – Bbbrrrr!"
5:   "BBBbrrrrroommmm!"
6:   "VVVvrrrrroommmm!"

Later Conversation:
1:   "Be quiet! Start off, Billy. What if you was the teacher?"
2:   "OK. If I was the teacher, I'd give us less work and more time to play – and I'd be mean to y'all too."
3:   "OK, Ann" (meaning that it is her turn).
4:   "If I was the teacher I'd do work – um. I'd sit around and watch T.V. I wouldn't assign no papers – umm ..."
5:   "I'd let y'all watch T.V. stories."
6:   "I'd turn the TV on channel 4 at 9:30 to watch *Popeye!*"

In the early conversation the participants respond to each other; however, they respond in terms of affect, not content, and they easily switch topics. Obviously guidance is needed in terms of topic selection. In the later conversation there is a topic, and it is not switched until the final utterance. Here guidance is needed in terms of thinking about why the children have chosen this topic and what their comments mean. Simply getting children to talk to each other does not further the *goals* of communication in the classroom such as enriching the topics of discussion, relating the topics to the curriculum in various areas, and increasing the complexity of sentence structure and vocabulary use. Table 5 presents an outline of possible school activities that can lead to further language development, literacy development, further subject matter understanding, and social development.

Development of Language Awareness and Reading

Schooling can be very important for the development of awareness of language categories and relations. The process of developing such awareness, as indicated previously, takes place in stages from intuitive knowledge to beginning awareness, as indicated by the ability to judge the correctness of categories and relations. Then awareness manifests itself by the ability to think out loud about categories and relations, usually in terms of providing examples of the structure in question. At this stage children can use this awareness automatically in germane situations such as listening, generating oral discourse, reading and

Table 5: Activities in school that lead to further language development.

Linguistic Process	Activities	Linguistic Outcomes	Social Outcomes	Subject Matter Application
Narration	Reading and telling stories (by teacher and by student)	Increased competence in all areas of language and literacy	--	Literature and History
Exposition and Explanation	Demonstration and explanation of projects by teacher and by student; Classroom interaction in problem solution	Increased competence in all areas of language and literacy	Learning to contribute, to process others' contributions, and to respond	Mathematics, science, social studies, literature (etc.)

writing. Later, children are not only aware of categories and relations in the language, but also able to talk about them.

A question that is often asked about linguistic awareness is: What is its importance? Certainly awareness of phonological categories and relations is required for decoding, a beginning stage of formal reading (Grimm and Skowronek, 1993). Awareness of other aspects of language also plays a role in reading: (1) in word recognition (for example, the word's syntactic role), (2) in sentence comprehension (relations among the words in the sentence), and (3) in discourse comprehension (relations among the sentences in the discourse). Writing requires awareness of all aspects of language in order to plan and produce a written piece. There also has to be awareness of the relation between oral language and written language (for example, the relation between phonology and orthography, or between syntax and punctuation).

Awareness also plays a role in the further development of language. There is a transitional period during which both new and old structures are used. For example, children in a transitional stage may exhibit both incorrect and correct use of past tense markers ("kissted" and "kissed"), or of relative clause pronouns ("the pajamas what my mommy bought me" and "the pajamas that my mommy bought me"). Becoming aware of the new structure leads to greater control of that structure, until errors are no longer made. To become a good speaker and writer, the child must be aware of lexical relations between words (synonyms, antonyms, similes and idioms) and semantactic relations among groups of words which helps in paraphrase (knowing different ways to say the same thing). Awareness is required in all aspects of editing, from word spelling to sentence construction to the organization of connected discourse.

Awareness in All Learning

Awareness of what you are doing whenever you try to learn new information or to solve problems saves time and leads to correct solutions. Becoming aware of what one is doing in any goal-oriented activity requires both knowledge of sequences of procedures and knowing when the goal has been achieved. For example, when adding three-digit numbers one must know a certain procedure to follow, and know to end when the third place is reached; when memorizing a list of words to remember for spelling, one may decide to rehearse the letters of the words until the list is completed. If the procedure is successful, it can be applied to other examples of the same kinds of problems (addition of other three-digit numbers, learning the spelling of a different list of words). In developmental psychology language, this awareness of the underlying process is called *meta-cognizing* and it allows transfer of learning. In this sense, meta-processing (or being aware of) is facilitative. In addition, frequent application of the process leads to automaticity; one doesn't need to think through application of the process in each instance. Once the process becomes automatic, the speed with which one carries out the process increases. When errors occur, awareness allows the thinker to review the application and determine where errors may have occurred. The ability to bring to conscious awareness what one knows about an area of application remains a useful and important tool in all learning situations.

Awareness of Language Categories

There are activities in school that develop awareness in all aspects of language. Some of these activities begin in the preschool years. As children are read to, or are beginning to read and write for themselves, they become aware of the relation between print and speech. Many prereading activities such as rhyming or attempting to spell words are the beginning stages of awareness of the phonology (speech)–orthography (print) relation. Later, children become aware of the relations between letters and the sounds in words, a giant step forward in the process of learning to read.

Awareness of the meanings of words and the relations among words can be taught in a number of differing ways. One common technique is to ask for definitions — but other strategies can be more helpful and provide better insights than simply requiring definitions. Many techniques that have been used in experiments to determine what children know about language and how they process language are good exercises in awareness. Very early on, at ages two to three years, when children are asked to group objects in different ways according to the labels provided (for example, "all animals" or "all furniture"), the results indicate that children have developed very good notions of what different words refer to. (Markman, 1991). Requiring children to group words that they think go together can be used with very young children, not only to examine their ability to understand reference but also, for example, to develop their awareness of superordinate ("put all the animals together") and subordinate ("put all the pets together") relations among words. Another activity that can help children at an early age to develop awareness of the derivation of words is to ask them to think about how different parts of speech compare to each other; e.g., how verbs such as *bake* compare to nouns such as *baker*. For older children, activities that call for comparisons across syntactic categories such as adjective-adverb (*quick* and *quickly*) and noun-adjective (*history* and *historical*) as well as verb–noun can be introduced.

A technique used by Werner and Kaplan (1950) with older children, to examine how they develop the meaning of a nonsense word through the verbal context in which it is placed, proved to be a very good technique for developing awareness of how verbal context can be used to derive meaning. The paper provides many examples of how this behavior can be elicited. The exercise might begin with a sentence such as "The flick was used by the gardener in his work" and continue with a sentence such as "The flick helped the gardener water the plants" and "The flick can be rolled up and stored." In this way the child can home in on the meaning of "flick" and learn that the meaning of words can be derived from contexts.

There are two factors that should be kept in mind when designing activities that help elicit awareness of the meanings of words.

(1) Techniques used to elicit understanding of word meaning should change as the children mature by altering the tasks and the contexts to match

their increased knowledge (target words and the sentence contexts in which they appear should increase in complexity).

(2) Efforts should be made to use techniques that are helpful in real-time discourse processing such as guessing the next word or phrase. Such activities help in reading as well, and in developing awareness of syntactic categories (what classes of words can follow others).

To develop awareness of semantactic relations in the language, grammar can be taught. Whether or not the grammar of the language should be taught has been a matter of some debate. The point may very well be not whether grammar should be taught, but *how* it should be taught. The groans that accompany requests to parse sentences could be avoided if semantax were taught by engaging children in the judgment of correct and incorrect sentences. This strategy allows them to puzzle out why some sentences are judged incorrect, while others that are quite similar, but not exactly alike, are judged correct. Children during this period can use their intuitive awareness to make these judgments. This awareness can be used to develop knowledge of semantic and syntactic relations in sentences, or grammar, as was discussed by Vygotsky (1962) many years ago, and used experimentally by a number of researchers. The technique involves two types of tasks: judgment of grammaticality and sentence completion. Some examples of the former are "He broke his leg because he went to the hospital"; "Before he opened the barn door, he was in the barn." These sentences are possible but unlikely and require some thought before a decision is made about grammaticality. Additional examples of these can be found in Flood and Menyuk (1983). Examples of a sentence completion task might include "Although John wanted to go to the movies ..." or "Because he went to the hospital ..." There have been many experiments that require meta-linguistic processing (bringing knowledge of language categories to awareness), and that have been or can be developed into activities that will help children achieve awareness of categories and relations in language. Further, these studies provide important data about the appropriate ages for the use of these tasks (since children of different ages have participated in the various studies) and how sociocultural or biological factors might affect performance on these tasks (since different populations of children have been used in these studies).

In two recent studies, my colleagues and I examined young children's ability to process and meta-process varying aspects of language (Menyuk et al., 1991; Menyuk & Chesnick, 1997). The purpose of the first study was to determine which language processing abilities at ages five to six were most predictive of eventual reading problems in a population of children considered "at risk." The definition of "at risk" was children who had language problems before school but on school entrance were largely functioning normally on language tests. The tasks used in that study examined processing abilities at the word, sentence, and connected-discourse levels. Since we compared the performance of normally developing and at-risk children, we discovered that not only did normally developing children do better than the at-risk children in all tasks, but that normally developing children continued to develop some of their meta-processing abilities over the three-year period of the study. The children at risk did so as well, but at a much slower rate. The second study focused on children with oral language, reading difficulties, or both, and was concerned with how we might get children with these problems to meta-process or bring to conscious awareness language categories and relations more efficiently.

The tasks used in both studies gave the children the opportunity to exercise their awareness of the language and, if they were unaware of an aspect of language, hopefully to develop such awareness. The findings of the second study, we thought, might be useful in determining the nature of the activities, the ages, and the conditions under which they could be presented to at-risk children as well as normally developing children. We also discovered that some of the meta-linguistic tasks we had developed needed to be adjusted so that a better awareness of a category or relation could be achieved.

Each of the tasks were designed to engage processing of different components of the language (speech sounds, words, sentences, and discourse). They were also chosen because they represent varying skills that are thought to be required in both reading and oral language processing: phoneme and syllable awareness, lexical categorization and retrieval, semantactic prediction, sentence analysis, and comprehension monitoring. The list of the tasks and a description of each follows. Included are comments about our findings and conclusions concerning the efficacy of the task. Each task is listed under a linguistic heading. The correlation between performance on these tasks and the children's performance on standard oral language and reading tests was measured throughout the age range (6 to 12 years) studied.

1. Phonological awareness. This was assessed by syllabic and phonological segmentation tasks which required the children to tap out the syllables or the phonemes in a list of words. Performance on these tasks was significantly related to reading and oral language development throughout the age range studied. However, simple segmentation of a word appears to be insufficient to probe phonological awareness of the composition of words. Upon further analysis, tasks which require the child to process the word when parts are removed or added (for example, "If we take away /s/ from stall, what's left?" or "If we take away /t/ from *meat*, what is left?") seem to elicit a deeper and possibly more useful awareness. Awareness of the syllabic composition of words can be easily elicited in normally developing first graders and even in those with language learning difficulties.

2. Lexical Awareness. Two tasks were presented to elicit lexical awareness. The first, *word recall*, was elicited by asking children to remember a group of 16 words, categorized into 4 subgroups with 4 items each (clothing, fruit, animals, furniture). The children were asked to name the pictures and given time to group the pictures. The pictures were then taken away and the children were asked to recall the names of the pictures. Our hypothesis was that to recall the words some form of rehearsal was used. We also assumed that grouping tapped awareness of word meaning, since a good way to remember would be by semantic classification. Thus, two forms of awareness of words, phonological through rehearsal and semantic through grouping, were being accessed in the task. Although this seems to be an appropriate conclusion, and the ability to recall words was significantly related to language development throughout the age range studied, we think it's an indirect method of tapping awareness of word meaning and that requiring word definition would be a more direct way to go. A still more interesting strategy to develop word retrieval is the oral cloze procedure discussed below and related to word accessing through sentence context discussed earlier.

In the second task, *rapid automatized naming*, the children were asked to name the first 5 pictures in a set. There were 4 sets (colors, numbers, objects and letters) and each set consisted of 5 different items randomly arranged in rows of 10 items. If the child could not supply the name, the name was given. They were then required to name items as quickly as possible until all items were named. We don't think that confrontation naming is the best way to elicit awareness of the meaning of words; however, performance on this task is significantly related to reading scores in older children, those aged 10 through 12. This may be because rapid naming or recognition of a word to get at the word's meaning is a crucial aspect of reading.

3. Semantactic Awareness. We administered three sentence processing tasks. In one, the *oral cloze task*, the experimenter indicated where a word was missing in a sentence by tapping, and asked the child to provide an appropriate word. One example is, "The [tap] tree was decorated." In another, the *complex sentence comprehension task*, the child answered questions about subjects and objects in embedded relative clause sentences, and answered questions about order of events in sentences using temporal terms. For example, upon hearing "The tiger chased by the lion climbed the tree," the child was asked who climbed the tree. In a third, a *grammaticality judgment task*, the child was required to indicate whether the sentence was right or wrong and to fix any sentence that was considered wrong. One example is, "I like the pajamas what my mom bought me." All three of these tasks, we believe, elicit semantactic awareness, and performance on all three tasks was significantly related to oral language development and reading throughout the age range of 7 to 12 years. However, we think not just accuracy but *rate* of processing, as in word retrieval, is a critical aspect in the relation between the linguistic processing in these tasks and reading.

4. Discourse Awareness. To elicit awareness of the units of a story, the children were asked to retell a story to a puppet and the number of propositions recalled as well as the order of recall was measured. This task was very significantly related to both oral language development and reading in the older children in the study, those aged roughly 10 to 12 years.

Some of the above tasks have been categorized as requiring bringing language categories to awareness (metalinguistic abilities), while others have not. Phonological segmentation, judgement and repair of sentences, and oral cloze have been deemed metalinguistic. Word recall, complex sentence comprehension, and story recall have not been considered as requiring metaprocessing; however, in our view, these latter tasks required organization of the material for recall and then later retrieval. We informed the children that they would be asked to recall words and sentences and answer questions about the sentences. Thinking about how to organize requires a certain level of metaprocessing. Automatic word recall is the one task that should not require metaprocessing if the words are well known. If they are not, there may be conscious search for the words initially, and automatic processing only subsequently.

In the second study, in addition to assessing awareness of the different aspects of language, various intervention procedures were used with these tasks to see if children with language problems, both oral and written, could improve their performance on these tasks over time. Some of the children in this study had problems in only one of these areas, as indicated by standard tests of oral language and reading. A vast majority had problems in both areas. The performance of children provided given help on the language processing tasks (experimental children) and that of children whose performance on these tasks were simply sampled periodically (control children) were compared. On the basis of past clinical and experimental studies, the researchers designed ways in which the children might be helped to encode (store) and retrieve (recall) the language categories (phonological, lexical, semantactic, and narrative) they were given. In general, these strategies focused on aiding the children's short-term memory by giving them cues for storage and retrieval. The altered encoding or storage conditions emphasized, organized, and/or repeated the linguistic information to be stored. The altered retrieval or recall conditions provided cues for recall of the linguistic information, or allowed comparison of the linguistic material that would aid in recall. These altered conditions are described in detail below. By showing them the way, we hoped to get the children to use these strategies spontaneously on subsequent occasions.

1. Phonological Segmentation. In the altered encoding condition for these tasks, the children watched the investigator divide the word into syllables or segments using visual stimuli, and then repeated the task independently. For example, for syllabic segmentation of the word *cantaloupe,* the investigator placed a blank card on the table for each syllable. For phoneme segmentation of the word *friend,* she did the same for each segment. The children were then asked to tap out the segments of the words in each list. In the retrieval condition the investigator orally segmented the word into syllables ("can-ta-loupe") or segments ("f-r-e-n-d") and asked the child to guess the word.

2. Semantactic Analysis. As stated, there were three semantactic analysis tasks. To help the child to accurately listen (to help in encoding) in the judgment of grammaticality task, the child first listened to a sentence presented orally, judged its grammaticality and repaired the sentence if needed. For incorrect responses, the examiner indicated what the right response was and the correction needed, thus focusing attention on particular structures. At the conclusion, these items were repeated for judgment and correction. In the recall (retrieval) condition, the child heard two sentences, one of which was correct, and had to choose the correct sentence. If the child made the wrong selection, the examiner presented the correct form, allowing comparison. After all the items had been presented, the incorrect items were repeated for re-evaluation and correction.

In the aided encoding condition (listening accurately) of the complex sentence comprehension task, the examiner read a sentence, stressed the salient word, and paused to allow more processing time. (For example, "My mother liked the *girl* ... who was carrying the big black suitcase. — Who was carrying the big black suitcase?"). This tactic, again, focused attention. If an error was still made, the investigator gave the correct answer. All sentences that elicited incorrect responses were repeated at the end of the task. In the retrieval (or recall) condition, after reading the sentence, the investigator provided two answers to the question put, and the child was to select the correct answer. This allowed for comparison. (For example, "The skinny lady saw the robber who was carrying a big bag. — Who was carrying the big bag, the robber or the skinny lady?"). Again, if any response was incorrect, the investigator gave the correct answer, and the sentences on which errors had been made were repeated at the end of the task.

In the oral cloze task, a single word was deleted from each sentence. The word was either a subject or object noun, a subject or object adjective, or a main verb. In the aided encoding condition of this task, the experimenter read the sentence which was missing a word, and tapped for the missing word. The sentence was then repeated slowly, and three words offered for the missing word (for example, "The [tap] tree was decorated. — The *fat, long,* or *Christmas* tree?"). The child was to select the correct word. In the retrieval condition, each sentence was presented in the same manner as in the encoding condition; that is, read with a tap in place of the missing word, and repeated slowly. The child was then asked a question that focused on the function of the missing word (e.g., "What kind of tree would be decorated?").

3. Lexical Retrieval. In both the aided encoding and retrieval conditions, the children were told that they would be given time to study the pictures, then the pictures would be removed, and they would be asked to remember the names of the pictures. In the aided encoding condition, the children looked at the pictures, sorted them into groups, and named the category. Help was given in categorization. They had one minute to study the pictures before they were removed. In the retrieval condition, the children named the pictures and were told that they could do anything with the pictures that would help them remember their names. Then they were given a two-minute study period before the pictures were removed and the children were asked to name as many pictures as they remembered. When a child could not name any more, the investigator would provide categorical cues such as "Can you name any more animals?"

In the aided encoding condition of the Rapid Autonomic naming tasks, the investigator provided an associative cue to each item to help in categorization. For example, in the color naming task, the experimenter pointed to items and said "Green—tree, orange—pumpkin," etc., and for the number task, "Two—eyes, seven—dwarfs," etc. The child was told to point to the item as it was named. A practice trial followed, and the child then named the array as rapidly as possible. In the retrieval condition the child was encouraged to take as much time as needed to name each item in the practice trial. If the child could not name the item, the experimenter provided a phonetic cue, i.e., the first sound of the word. The child was then asked to name the items as quickly as possible.

4. Discourse Recall. In the discourse recall task a story was presented in episodes. After each episode the children were asked questions about what they thought had occurred and what they inferred might happen next.

When the performance of the experimental and the control children were compared periodically and over time, it was found that the experimental children improved significantly more rapidly over time than the control children in processing the material; that is, the help we provided significantly improved the performance of the children. Those aids that were particularly helpful were those provided for the phonological tasks, the sentence judgment task, and the oral cloze task. The aids provided for automatic word retrieval — semantic associations or phonological cuing — were not particularly helpful. If the tasks were revised, and word retrieval examined under more natural conditions such as in providing definitions or (even more appropriately) retrieval in sentences, the intervention might be found to be more helpful.

The results of our study indicate that opportunities to focus on particular aspects of language within the stream of speech may be of particular importance to children with language learning problems. Presenting aspects of language in ways that isolate these aspects and provide memory aids to the children can be beneficial in developing awareness of these aspects. The memorial aids are of different kinds. Modeling possible answers or the correct answer is one. Repetition of sentences with appropriate phrasing and stress is another tactic for highlighting what should be attended to. Providing semantic or functional cues for retrieval is another. Given the fact that children with language problems are integrated into classrooms, it becomes particularly important to develop techniques within the classroom that can be of help to these children. Further, many students in classrooms who have not been identified as having a language problem might benefit from these types of interventions as well.

In summary, studies of what children know about language at various ages often provide us with possible and interesting techniques for generating metalinguistic processing in children. Other studies which examine what children can learn about language at various ages provide us with possible and interesting techniques for enhancing and elaborating metalinguistic abilities in children in all domains of language. Some language processing tasks provide students with valuable experience in thinking about and expressing their thoughts about linguistic categories and relations. These abilities, for the most part, develop naturally over time, and are aided by learning to read. However, some of the activities described can make all children more expert in their use of language for academic purposes, and help some children who are in particular need of help to do so. Table 6 on the next page provides a list of activities that may be helpful in developing awareness of language categories and relations, and also, learning and memory strategies.

Language Delay and Language Difference

One needs also to keep in mind differences among normally developing children in terms of their readiness to take on specific metalinguistic tasks. As was stated at the beginning of this section, children are able to become aware of different aspects of language as they acquire knowledge of these aspects of language. A child cannot become aware of what he or she does not yet know.

We have discussed differences between normally developing children and those with problems in language development. Individual variation in the language abilities of children is a fact that teachers have always had to consider and attempt to deal with. However, two new factors have more dramatically affected the variation within classrooms over the past decade than in the previous ones. The first is the increasing number of children who come to school speaking a language other than English, and the move to maintain their own cultural and linguistic differences as well as joining into the mainstream soci-

Table 6: Development of language awareness and use

Bringing to Awareness Other Knowledge than Language Alone		
Processes	*Activities*	*Outcomes*
Awareness of Other Kinds of Knowledge (with Language as the Medium)	Awareness of strategies to solve problems; Awareness of strategies to remember categories and sequences; Awareness in planning oral and written discourse	Literacy, reading; using language to learn and remember
Bringing to Awareness All Aspects of Language		
Aspects of Language	*Processes and Activities*	
Phonological Awareness	Phonology: Awareness of segments in words. Exs: Tap out sounds in "stick"; Take away syllable or sound ("window" > "dow", "stick" > "tick")	
Semantactic Awareness	Awareness of relations in sentences. Exs: Fill in blanks in "The ___ boy sat on the ___ bench"; Judgment of Grammaticality of "There's three trees there"; Who/what is the subject of the main clause "The tiger the lion chased ran into the forest"?	
Morphological Awareness	Exs: "I see a wug — Here are two (wugs)"; History is part of our ____ heritage, He is glane so he has ____, Some people are ruly and some are ____.	
Discourse Awareness	Exs: "What are the main points in this story/ explanation?"; "What is a good title for this story/explanation?"; "There are mistakes in this story/explanation—fix them."	

ety. During previous waves of immigration, primarily during the beginning of the 20th century, many of the children of immigrant families did not attend school, or the focus was on integrating as quickly as possible.

The second factor is the movement of children with special needs to the regular classroom, a process called inclusion. Many of these children have particular difficulties with language, both oral and written. These are clear examples of variation that should impact the design of curricula to enhance language development and awareness. Of course, there are also differences among normally developing children in terms of their readiness to handle language related academic tasks. Table 7 outlines some of the sources of variation that can lead to differences in readiness for these activities.

Table 7: Possible sources of variation in language development.

I.   Input factors
     A.   Nature of language interation
     B.   Topics of discourse
     C.   Various uses of language
II. Different languages and dialects
     A.   Slower development of second or mainstream language
     B.   Differences in uses of language
     C.   Nature of language interaction
     D.   Topics of discourse
III. Psychobiological factors: language delay and disorder
     A.   Slower development of language due to
          1.   Rate of processing
          2.   Form of storage of grammatical knowledge
          3.   Organization of connected discourse
     B.   Slower development of reading
     C.   Slower development of awareness of language

Children who enter school with native competence in a language other than English might have their initial language experiences in either two-way bilingual classrooms (some children learning their language while they learn English). If this is not possible, programs that allow time for presentation of tasks in their native language and in English can be helpful. What is interesting about second language acquirers is that the process of second language acquisition can make them initially more aware of language categories and relations. In a number of studies bilingual children have been found to achieve awareness of aspects of language earlier then monolingual children (Menyuk, 1988, chapter 11).

Children who speak a language other than that of the classroom can also vary from native speakers of English in the ways in which they use language, not just in structural knowledge. As was discussed earlier, different sociolinguistic groups may have very different notions about the use of language (Heath, 1983). They may, unlike middle-class American-English-speaking children, use means other than language to remember, learn, and problem-solve, and therefore they may need another approach to carry out these activities. Further, sometimes it is difficult to distinguish language difference from language delay and disorder. There are, of course, also children who know another language and have had difficulties in acquiring that language — thus they are both language-different *and* language-delayed or -disordered.

Although different children come to school knowing different languages, there are few tools to assess the presence or absence of a language delay or disorder. It is easier to detect the difference between children who know little English because they have had little exposure to the language, and children who are native speakers of English but because of varying developmental disabilities do not know as much about English as most of the other native speakers in the classroom. Background information collected from the family and medical and school records of marked delay in development or a history of serious illness can and should play an important role in identifying children with language problems. In summary, there are individual differences in rate of language development in native English-speaking children. There can be marked differences among the normally developing children in the classroom because of differences in exposure to the language of the classroom, different experiences in the use of language, and biological differences that can affect the rate of learning. In any individual child these differences might be compounded.

Several suggestions have been made to overcome some of these problems by planning an effective curriculum for language development. All of these need further examination in order to understand how the presentation of particular language experiences benefit all children. One of the outstanding current needs is adequate assessment of the language knowledge and use of language by all the children in the classroom. The term *authentic assessment* has been used to describe evaluations of children as they are engaged in learning. Knowing how much a child can learn and under what conditions provides enormously useful cues for the design of curriculum for small groups of children as well as individuals. However, even if the children are adequately assessed, there are still questions that arise about how their language knowledge and use should affect the curriculum. These questions appear to fall into two large categories. The first category centers around children with language knowledge other than English. The question is, what language should the children be taught in and when? This is the "bilingual education" question; there are many ongoing discussions about whether children should be taught in their non-

English native language initially and then later in English, or taught in both simultaneously as is suggested in this work, or simply immersed in English. The second category of question has to do with the conditions under which the types of language activities discussed in this paper should be presented to children who vary markedly in their language learning abilities, the so-called inclusion or non-inclusion model.

These questions have often been studied as if they were simple, and they are not. For example, although much current data indicates that children need to be exposed to academic subjects in the language they are most familiar with, other data point to the enhancement of metalinguistic abilities by learning more than one language (Bialystok, 1991). Alternative models such as two-way bilingual programs, in which all children in a classroom are learning a second language and being simultaneously taught academic subjects in a native language, need to be tested. It has been found that children from a variety of socioeconomic as well as linguistic backgrounds can benefit from learning a language other than their own during the early school years (Genessee, 1985).

Recent research also indicates the positive effects of having children of differing levels of competence participate jointly in academic programs. Peer tutoring or peer teaching has been pointed to as one of the factors which may bring about greater success for children with special needs if they are included in regular classrooms. Another positive aspect of inclusion that has been found is the advantage to a majority of the children in the classroom of presenting language material in ways which (a) give them greater time for processing and (b) require bringing to awareness what is known rather than relying solely on rapid automatic processing. Many of the tasks described in the section on metaprocessing of different aspects of language were designed specifically for children who are delayed in language development. Clearly, how children fare under these circumstances needs to be continuously assessed. Inclusion may bring about the desired results for all the children in the classroom or for only some of the children, and alternative models need to be investigated. Again, the circumstances under which particular children learn best needs to be determined.

Earlier there was some discussion about the effect of maturation on language development, as well as the effect of schooling. It was pointed out that although certain aspects of language knowledge and processing need time to develop, schooling can enhance and elaborate on this knowledge. The child becomes an expert in language through the combined processes of schooling and maturation. It is clear that not all children become experts in language knowledge and use. Some children have an even more difficult time in becoming expert than others, but it is evident that certain kinds of experiences in school can enhance the learning of all children.

Chapter Three

Language Development Over the Later School Years: Curriculum Development

Language development over the later school years (approximately from 11 to 18 years) becomes more and more a product of what has been acquired by this time and further schooling. Language knowledge, like any other kind of knowledge, builds on what is already known. However, there is mounting evidence that the notion of a "critical period" of language development being passed at this age for both first- and second-language acquisition is open to question. A number of studies have found that children in the early high school years learn aspects of a second language more rapidly than do younger children and adults when all are learning language in a classroom.

At this stage developments continue to occur in all aspects of language: morphophonological (not simply phonological), lexical, semantactic, and discourse. Most of these developments are elaborations on what is already known and, also, on awareness of the linguistic knowledge that has been acquired. These elaborations and the development of awareness are important in the children's development of communicative competence, and certainly have an effect on academic achievement. Developments during this period in all aspects will be described.

Morphophonology

In morphophonological development, the aspect that develops is derivation of words by elaborating on roots and increasing awareness of the relation among root words and their derivations. This was previously referred to as suffixing (*bake–baker*), prefixing (*agree–disagree*), and infixing (*discuss–discussion*, *address* (noun)–*address* (verb), etc.). Three kinds of knowledge of morphophonology develop over this period. The first is simply an expansion of vocabulary as children acquire knowledge of more and more words. The second is awareness of the relation between the root word and a derivation in any instance (the root and its suffix, prefix, or infix; e.g., the relation between *history* and *historical*). Third, children become aware of the relations among types of suffixes, prefixes, and infixes; in other words, they learn the rules (for example, the similarity between *address* noun and verb, *contract* noun and verb, etc.).

Not all children achieve this last awareness, which appears to be largely a product of education. In studies that have examined children's knowledge of these relations, marked differences have been found due to the level of education of the subjects in these studies. This may be related to reading, or to the type of reading the student engages in. The symbiotic relation between reading and language development becomes increasingly evident over these later school years. It was observed by Myerson (1975) that there is a relation between reading competence and awareness of the derivational rules of the language. There is also a development over time in the types of derivational rules that children become aware of.

Semantax

Semantax rules that are acquired during this period of development appear to be a function of the kinds of verbs that are increasingly used and the structures that these verbs take. Mental verbs such as *know* and *think* are acquired and frequently used at an earlier age. These verbs take complement structures as in the following sentences.

1. I know that he will come.
2. I think that he will come.

In the early school years children not only use these verbs but they also understand the implications of their meanings. That is, they can distinguish the meaning of *know* versus *think* in terms of the speaker's certainty about whether the person "he" will come. During this period the child begins to use verbs such as *promise, expect,* and *asked* with greater frequency, and these verbs take the following kinds of complements.

3. Jim promised Bill to go to the movies with him.
4. Jim expected Bill to go to the movies with him.

5. Jim asked Bill to go to the movies with him

In sentence 3 the meaning is that the subject of the main sentence, *Jim,* is probably going to go to the movies. In 4, the object of the main sentence, *Bill,* is probably going to go to the movies, and in sentence 5 it is not clear whether the object *Bill* will go to the movies or not. These differences in use of verbs indicate two things. First, children are better able to use more syntactically complex structures, that is, those in which the first noun isn't always the subject of the verb. Second, children are increasingly able to express meanings that are more uncertain and abstract.

During this period there is not only an increasing use by some children of the above types of structures, but also an awareness that sentence 5 is ambiguous concerning the outcome. Children become increasingly aware of the role that these less frequent types of verbs can play in varying sentence structures. When asked to think about these varying roles (as in sentence completion tasks), they then can become adept at using these structures in their writing. Some children also become increasingly aware of the underlying structure of paraphrased sentences and ambiguous sentences. If they are given the task of providing underlying meanings for these two types of structures, they are able to do so. Sentences 6 and 7 below are paraphrases of each other; sentence 8 is an ambiguous sentence; sentences 9 and 10 are possible meanings for ambiguous sentence 8.

6. Mary sent Joe a valentine.
7. Joe was sent a valentine by Mary.
8. Bill believes that he is sick.
9. Bill believes that someone is sick.
10. Bill believes himself to be sick.

The frequency of use of complement structures of the types described in sentences 3 through 5 increases during this period. Awareness of the underlying structure of paraphrases and ambiguous sentences appears during this period. Further, there is a relation between awareness of ambiguity and paraphrase and competence in reading (Flood & Menyuk, 1983). This relation exists from 4th grade on through freshman year in college. The question arises again, whether being a good reader leads to this further knowledge of the semantax of the language, or vice versa. Historical data from populations that do not read but are still able to generate semantactically highly complex sentences (for example, the storytelling of non-literate Native Americans) suggest that such knowledge can be developed without written representations. But, again, advanced developments in oral language knowledge and more competent reading appear to go together. That is, reading such structures does not lead to oral language knowledge and awareness, but such knowledge and awareness makes comprehension of such structures in text possible and the reading process more automatic. The chicken-or-egg question does not arise in the area of writing. Increased awareness of these structures in oral language leads to better writing; that is, these structures can make writing much more compact and interesting.

Lexicon

Lexical development, of course, continues throughout one's lifetime, so of course it continues through this period. In the elementary school years, many of the new words acquired were generated by application of morphophonological derivational rules. This development accounts for the very steep rise in number of words known between first and fifth grade. During this period, lexical development is not simply a matter of new words being acquired. Children acquire knowledge of double meanings for words, idioms, similes, metaphors, that is, so-called figurative language. This knowledge appears to be principally acquired from two sources. One, of course, is reading; the other is listening and using one's semantax knowledge to figure out the underlying meanings for such figurative language. In an earlier period the child is very literal in the translation of such idioms as "He kicked the bucket," but he or she is listening to how these are used in the language. The child listens to sayings such as "Every dog has his day," "Roses are red, violets are blue, sugar is sweet and so are you," and expressions such as "He really is a dog" and "She is a sweet person." It is from these sources that double or connotative as well as denotative meanings for words are acquired. Lexical acquisition, like semantax acquisition, involves both acquisition of new knowledge, elaboration of old, and awareness of multiple meanings. Clearly, familiarity with and use of figurative language can dramatically affect writing, and make it more interesting and meaningful.

Discourse

The most obvious language development that occurs during this period is the maturation of conversational competence and connected discourse. It is during this period that the child learns how to effectively participate in conversations, how to tell cohesive stories, and how to provide descriptions and explanations. Clearly the growth of these abilities is a function of increasing linguistic competence. For example, children are much better story tellers than they were previously because, for one thing, they learn how to correctly use anaphoric devices — using pronouns and other structures that provide reference while eliminating the need for repetition. A story such as "The boy and the squirrel were friends. He went into the forest to find nuts, and he found them." changes to "A boy and a squirrel were friends. They went into the forest to find nuts and the squirrel found them." Sentences such as "George plays the piano and Margaret does so too" become more frequent. Children throughout this developmental period become much better describers and explainers because they have more complex semantax and richer lexical knowledge available. The following example is a conversation among high schoolers. Again, the data come from Dorval & Eckerman (1984). These are unguided conversations, therefore, the topic was selected by the participants and was unmonitored. (The numbers before utterances indicates the turn in the conversation.)

1. Sandy, she was really — y'know — she said she argued with her mother an'...
2. Her mother's attitude was that she'd disgraced the family, you know. And she was shocked 'cause she's so religious herself.
3. She's so self-righteous. She ...
4. Her attitude was part of the problem — why Sandy left school and all.
5. Why'd she leave school anyway?

Changes in turn-taking abilities, changes in making responses more contingent on the previous utterance, and changes in topic have all occurred by this time.

In addition to developments in story telling and conversational abilities, there are also marked changes in the children's abilities to present explanations, descriptions, and arguments. The sequential pattern of stories and the contingent pattern of responses in conversations need to be replaced by main ideas and subsidiary ideas in such explanations, descriptions and arguments.

The ability to outline their thinking into these main and subsidiary ideas affects the quality of their presentations.

Curriculum Suggestions

In all subject areas, there are opportunities that engage the student in both oral and written practice in story telling, conversational interaction, and generation of explanations, descriptions, and argument. However, these opportunities need to be planned and guided. Planning for participation in these activities is not an easy task because individual differences in student competence and interests become even more marked in these later grades. Developing curriculum materials that span the disciplines is a challenging task, but it can have remarkable payoff in terms of offering a multiplicity of opportunities for students to engage in continuous practice in these activities in each of the subject areas.

Language differences and problems

As noted previously, there are a number of sources for differences in language development that can affect school performance. The principal sources for these differences can be found in Table 7. Some of these sources of differences need not affect language development throughout the school years; they can be dealt with early on. Under I in table 7, such differences as limited topics of discourse, types of language interaction, and uses of language in the home can be dealt with early on in school. However, the attitude needs to be that these differences among children are amenable to changes if educational programs are designed to bring about these changes — not that these children are condemned to poor academic performance and illiteracy because of background differences. Further, in cooperation with families, changes can be carried out in the home as well as school. Early educational interventions such as Head Start programs provide some evidence for this. The sources of differences indicated under heading II in Table 7 are differences in early linguistic experiences from children who use the non-mainstream language. Although much research still needs to be done to find the most effective ways to make these children competent in all their languages (and dialects), much has already been done to point the way to effective programs such as early two-way bilingual programs, and more schools are exposing children to a second language early on, in first grade or even kindergarten.

To help children whose development has been affected by psychobiological factors particular interventions that allow them to process language, as well as other sources of information, more effectively need to be designed. One possible intervention that appears to aid these children to become more aware of parts of the language was described in this monograph. Making them more aware of parts of language we believe will help them in reading and oral language development. Some of them need this support throughout the school years as academic tasks become more complicated. Those without these problems will need continuous stimulation so they can engage in more and more complex activities outlined above during the differing periods of development. Students with psychobiological problems also need continuous stimulation as well as special conditions for encoding and processing this information. The rate at which information is presented and responses required is just one difference in conditions of learning that may exist for these children.

References

Anglin, J. (1993). Vocabulary development: A morphological analysis. *Monographs of the Society for Research in Child Development,* Serial No. 238, Vol. 58, No. 10.

Berko-Gleason, J. (1958). The child's learning of English morphology. *Word, 14,* 150-177.

Bialystok, E. (Ed.) (1991). *Language processing in bilingual children.* Cambridge, UK: Cambridge University Press.

Berman, R., & Slobin, D. (Eds.) (1994). *Relating events in narrative.* Mahwah, NJ: Lawrence Erlbaum Associates, Inc.

Cazden, C., Cox, M., Dickinson, D., Steinberg, Z., & Stone, C. (1978). "You all gonna hafta listen": Peer teaching in a primary classroom. In W. Collins (Ed.), *Children's language and communication* (12th Annual Minnesota Symposium on Child Development), pp. 183-231. Hillsdale, NJ: Erlbaum Associates, Inc.

Case, R., & Okamoto, Y. (1996) The role of central conceptual structures in the development of children's thought. *Monographs of the Society for Research in Child Development,* Vol. 61, Serial No. 246.

Dorval, B., & Eckerman, C. (1984). Developmental trends in the quality of conversation achieved by small groups of acquainted peers. *Monographs of the Society for Research in Child Development,* Vol. 29, No. 2, Serial No. 206.

Edwards, D. (1993). But what do children really think? Discourse analysis and conceptual content in children's talk. *Cognition and Instruction, 11,* 207-225.

Fenson, L., Dale, P., Reznick, J., Thal, D., Baks, F., & Hartung, J. (1993). *MacArthur communicative development inventories.* San Diego, CA: Singular.

Flood, J., & Menyuk, P. (1983) The development of metalinguistic awareness and its relation to reading. J. *Applied Developmental Psychology, 4,* 65-80.

Flavell, J. (1985). Cognitive development. Englewood Cliffs, NJ: Prentice-Hall, Inc.

Genesee, F. (1985). Second-language learning through immersion: A review of United States programs, *Review of Educational Research, 55,* 541-561.

Genesee, F. (1989). Early bilingual development: One language or two? *Journal of Child Language, 16,* 161-180.

Gleitman, L., Gleitman, H., & Shipley, E. (1972). The child as a grammarian. *Cognition, 1,* 137-164.

Grimm, H., & Skowronek, H. (1993). *Language acquisition problems and reading disorders: Aspects of diagnosis and intervention.* Berlin: Walter de Gruyter.

Homza, A. (1995) *Developing biliteracy in a bilingual first grade writing work shop.* Unpublished doctoral dissertation, Boston University.

Heath, S.B. (1983) *Ways with words.* Cambridge, UK: Cambridge University Press.

Hickmann, M. (1985), The implications of discourse skills in Vygotsky's developmental theory.

In J. Wertsch (Ed.), *Culture, communication and cognition* (pp. 236-257). Cambridge, UK: Cambridge University Press.

Karmiloff-Smith, A. (1986). From meta-process to conscious awareness: Evidence from children's metalinguistic and repair data. *Cognition, 23,* 95-147.

Krashen, S. (1996). *Under attack: The case against bilingual education.* Culver, CA: Language Education Associates.

MacWhinney, B. (1978). The acquisition of morphophonology. *Monographs Society for Research in Child Development,* Vol. 43, Serial No. 174.

Markman, E. (1991). The whole-object, taxonomic, and mutual exclusivity assumptions as initial constraints on word meanings. In S. Gelman & J. Byrnes (Eds.), *Perspectives on language and thought: Interrelations in development* (pp. 72-106). Cambridge, UK: Cambridge University Press.

Menyuk, P. (1991). Metalinguistic abilities and language disorder. In J. Miller (Ed.), *Research on child language disorders: A decade of progress* (pp. 387-398). Austin, TX: Pro-Ed.

Menyuk, P. (1988). *Language development: Knowledge and use.* New York: HarperCollins.

Menyuk, P. (1984). Language development and reading. In J. Flood (Ed.), *Understanding reading comprehension* (pp. 101-121). Newark, DE: International Reading Association.

Menyuk, P., & Chesnick, M. (1997). Metalinguistic skills, oral language knowledge, and reading. *Topics in Language Disorder, 17,* 75-89.

Menyuk, P., Chesnick, M., Liebergott, J., Korngold, B., D'Agostino, R., & Belanger, A. (1991). Predicting reading problems in at-risk children. *Journal of Speech and Hearing Research, 34,* 893-903.

Mishler, E. (1975). Implications of teachers' strategies for language and cognition. In C. Cazden, V. Johns, & D. Hymes (Eds.), *Functions of language in the classroom.* New York: Teachers College Press.

Myerson, R. (1976). *A study of children's knowledge of certain word formation rules and the relationship of this knowledge to various forms of reading complex derived words of English.* Unpublished doctoral dissertation, Harvard University, Cambridge, MA.

Paul, R., Muncy, C., Clancy, K., & D. Andrews (1997). Reading and metaphonological outcomes for late talkers. *Journal of Speech, Language and Hearing Research, 40,* 1037-1047.

Perfetti, C., & McCutchen (1987). Schooled language competence: Linguistic abilities in reading and writing. In S. Rosenberg (Ed.), *Advances in applied psycholinguistics,* Vol. 2 (pp. 105-141). Cambridge, UK: Cambridge University Press.

Piaget, J. (1970). Piaget's theory. In P. Mussen (Ed.), *Manual of child psychology VI* (pp. 705-730). New York: Wiley.

Pinker, S. (1994). *The language instinct: How the mind creates language.* New York: Morrow.

Pinker, S. (1984). *Language learnability and language development.* Cambridge, MA: Harvard University Press.

Rescorla, L., Roberts, J., & Dahlsgaard, K. (1997). Late talkers at 2: Outcome at age 3. *Journal of Speech, Language, and Hearing Research, 40,* 556-566.

Richgels, D., McGee, L., Lomax, R., & Sheard, C. (1987). Awareness of four text structures: Effects on recall of expository text. *Reading Research Quarterly, 2,* 177- 193.

Roberts, J. Sanyal, M., & Burchinal, M. (1986). Otitis media in early childhood and its relationship to late verbal-academic performance. *Pediatrics, 78,* 423-430.

Schieffelin, B., & Ochs, E. (1986). *Language socialization across cultures.* New York: Cambridge University Press.

Siegler, R. (1991). *Children's thinking.* Englewood Cliffs, NJ: Prentice-Hall, Inc.

Teale, W., & Sulzby, E. (1986). *Emergent literacy.* Norwood, NJ: Ablex.

Templin, M. (1957). *Certain language skills in children: Their development and interrelationships.* Institute of Child Welfare, Monograph Series No. 26. Minneapolis: University of Minnesota Press.

Vellutino, F. (1979). *Dyslexia: Theory and research.* Cambridge, MA: The MIT Press.

Vygotsky, L. (1962). *Thought and language.* Cambridge, MA: The MIT Press.

Wells, G. (1983). Talking with children: The complementary roles of parents and teachers. In M. Donaldson, R. Grieve, & C. Pratt (Eds.), *Early childhood development and education.* New York: The Guilford Press.

Werner, H., & Kaplan, E. (1950). Development of word meaning through verbal context: An experimental study. *Journal of Psychology, 29,* 251-257.

About the Author

Paula Menyuk is Professor Emerita of Education at Boston University. She specializes in the study of the development of children's language and the consequences of deviant language acquisition on school and non-school performance.